# Get Cleansed and Fill Your Lamp With Oil
### (Revised Edition)

*Includes 30-Day Self-help Pages*

Christy Tola

Contains Divine Guides for
Various Life Situations

Copyright © 2014 Christy Tola
Get Cleansed and Fill Your Lamp With Oil
(Revised Edition)

Includes 30-Day Self-help Pages
Contains Divine Guides for Various Life Situations

All rights reserved under International Copyright Law. Contents and/or Cover may not be reproduced in whole or part in any form without the written consent of the Publisher.

Library of Congress Number: 2013935785
ISBN: 9789729240355

All Scriptures Quotations are taken from the New King James Version of the Bible.

Part of the Proceeds Will Go Towards Talent Awareness Program for Youth & Unemployed Graduates.

Christy Tola Arts & Books
P O Box 4243
Oak Park
IL 60304. USA.

# Table of Contents

## Introduction 5

## Chapter 1
### Unholy Exposures 8

## Chapter 2
### The Power of the Scriptures 26

## Chapter 3
### The Power of Praise & Worship 43

## Chapter 4
### The Importance of God's Presence 51

## Chapter 5
### Divine Guides for Handling Some Life Situations 54

# Chapter 6

## Conclusion 90

## Is Your Soul Saved? 95

## Prayer Points 101

## Self-help Pages 107

## Contact Details 137

## *Introduction*

This book provides divine answers to some questions that many people have been asking concerning the disturbing and unpleasant situations that are currently going on in the world.

It also provides divine solutions for those going through spiritual afflictions, as well as spiritual guides on how we can be protected from our spiritual enemies.

Lastly, it's to alert Christians to the spiritual consequences that can occur, if they are inconsistent with their Bible Study, Praise, Worship, and Prayers.

Unclean spirits are spiritual contaminants to Human Souls and have various ways of creating openings in their victim's lives. Their aims are to prevent God's children from hearing His voice, alienate them from His Presence, as well as deprive them of His protection. The truth is that, many of God's children cannot fulfill their divine purpose the way they should, if they are not under the guidance and protection of God. This is because His Presence will help them to hear His voice and shield them from their enemies, while they are serving Him.

Over the years, God has given me various opportunities, (some through spiritual afflictions), to experience the Power of the Scriptures, Praise, Worship and Prayers. The experiences have also helped me to find out that God's spiritual Oil of Joy, the Anointing, released when we enter His Presence, is the means by which He sanctifies, nourishes, rejuvenates and protects us, as well as fills our void.

Let's imagine this; if every single person on Earth can enter God's Presence when they worship, more of His Anointing will be released, which is what the World really needs at this time. All the changes that we want around us will come through the changes that we are able to make individually as a result of our relationship with God.

Before you continue reading, if you do not know the Lord, please say the prayer below because you need the help of the Holy Spirit:

*Dear Heavenly Father, I am sorry for my sins. Please forgive me. I now accept Jesus Christ as my Lord and Savior. Let Your Holy Spirit come into my life and reveal my Divine Purpose and let the eyes of my spiritual understanding be opened to the truth in this book. In Jesus name. Amen.*

It's my prayer that you will be given a heart of obedience to follow God's Instructions and study the Scriptures more. Please endeavor to worship God daily, so that you will be filled with His Oil of Joy, healed in your Body and Soul, be happy, protected, enjoy life the way you should, and fulfill your divine purpose in life. In Jesus name. Amen.

*"It shall come to pass in that day That his burden will be taken away from your shoulder, And his yoke from your neck, And the yoke will be destroyed because of the anointing oil"* Isaiah 10:27.

May the Lord bless you richly.

Christy Tola.

# Chapter One
## *Unholy Exposures*

Many people are born with God's Divine Power. The degree of His Power in those born as such, depends on the nature of their divine assignment in life.

Because many of God's people lack the necessary Anointing, which is generated when they read the Scriptures and worship, their spiritual enemies are able to see His Light and Power at work in their lives. As a result, many of them have been subjected to spiritual attacks.

Also, as a result of some people's exposure to unclean spirits, these spiritual enemies have craftily enticed them to do things that will make them to become further exposed to spiritual contaminations. This is because they know that those who are in such state cannot enter God's Presence, where they will be able to obtain the necessary help that will aid and guide them towards fulfilling their divine assignments in life, as well as draw the Holy Spirit close to them.

Furthermore, those that are born with God's Divine Power are targeted and afflicted before they can come to the realization of who they are, and the great mission(s) that they are supposed to accomplish during their lifetime.

It's important to note that, because those that are seriously affected due to exposure to spiritual uncleanness do not have the Anointing that is supposed to protect and help them to be spiritually strong, as well as counter the effects of exposure to unclean spirits, the resultant spiritual weakness has led some of them to commit evil acts. This is because they have become easy target for their spiritual enemies to manipulate their minds and has resulted in many of the abominable crimes that we see in our communities today. *If spiritual laws are broken, strange things will happen.*

Furthermore, it's unfortunate that many of those affected have succumbed to their afflictions. This is evident in some of those that are sad and depressed and are currently undergoing counseling, or admitted to various rehabilitation centers, or in those that are incapacitated. Sadly, it has resulted in the demise of some.

It's my prayer that God will open the spiritual eyes of those that are currently in the above predicaments to see the divine solutions around them and deliver them from evil traps. If the Reader relates to this situation, it's important that you read the Scriptures (especially the Psalms), and worship God whenever evil or suicidal thoughts are coming to your mind, or you suddenly become sad or depressed. (Please see Guide 'J' in Chapter 5 for relevant Scriptures and other important information).

The second important reason for the exposure to unclean spirits is the Media. Most of what we see in the media today has created spiritual openings for unclean spirits to come into people's lives. Those that are mostly affected are young people who are indoor most of the time, and their main companions are their media devices, which has become addictive to a lot of them. It's my prayer that the spiritual eyes of understanding of many people will be enlightened by this truth.

I must say that there is absolutely nothing wrong in being entertained by some of today's media devices, but it's important for people to know that if certain kinds of games are played repeatedly (mostly violent and ritual-based games), they will create openings for enemies to come into the lives of those playing them. Once the unclean spirits are in, they will have access to the person's mind and control their lives. Unless something is done immediately after playing the game(s), what they don't want to see happen, is likely to happen to some of them in future. Best if they can avoid some of the games completely.

The spiritual anti-dote to spiritual uncleanness is to read, confess or listen to some Scriptures (especially Psalms), and Gospel Worship Music, immediately after playing violent and ritual-based games. (Please see Chapter 5 Guide 'K').

The fervent prayers of some relatives and friends of many young people are what God is using to protect them. If you have been praying, please don't stop. Continue to pray for those that are vulnerable among your relatives and friends and God will surely reward your efforts.

*"For God is not unjust to forget your work and labor of love which you have shown toward His name, in that you have ministered to the saints…"*

Hebrews 6:10.

## Spiritual Implications

Let's look at some spiritual implications of the above issues discussed. As spiritual beings living in physical bodies, we must be very careful. This is because of the Divine Nature that we share with God.

*"You are gods..."* Psalm 82:6.

The repetitive nature of what some people are engaging themselves in, either through watching violent games and movies, or confessing lyrics or words with evil incantations, will result in spiritual seed (which are impure in nature), to be formed in their lives. When seed are sown, whether good or bad, harvest is expected to follow.

*"...Whatever a man sows, that he will also reap"*
Galatians 6:7.

To a great extent, we have power to create, just as God, because He has given us dominion over many things. In Genesis Chapter 1, God spoke things into existence-*" Let there be..."* If God created with *"Let there be..."*, and commanded us to go and subdue the earth, then He has invested and imparted authority and power into us (Genesis Chapter 1:28).

Also, we are referred to as *"gods" in* Psalm 82:6. Therefore, there is power in our confession and we have the ability to do great exploits (Daniel 11:32). But many people (though unknowingly), are using their God-given Power to do or create the wrong things or situation for themselves, many of which cannot be undone. What they do not realize is that their Divine Power will heed their commands.

It's also important to note that the repetitive nature of the unholy things that some have exposed themselves to or have participated in, have made their hearts to become hardened (Ephesians 4:18) and the consequence is that they can no longer hear or perceive the *'still small voice'* of God (1 Kings 19:12), which is supposed to help prevent them from doing things that they are not supposed to do.

As said earlier, God has been using the prayers and worship of some individuals, as well as some Churches/Ministries, to continue to protect people and keep many places clean and together.

If the Reader is identified with the issue discussed so far, it's time to do things differently. Instead of repeating certain kinds of games that are unhealthy for your spiritual well-being, you should begin to substitute them with good and creative games or engage yourself more in your God-given talents or God's work, such as charitable activities. This will activate God's Divine Power in you to create or invent good and new things that will bless and help you, and the society. Always remember that the divine nature in us is holy and pure;

> *"You are a chosen generation, a royal priesthood, a holy nation..."* 1 Peter 2:9.

To parents of young people, I will suggest that you should prayerfully persuade your children to substitute some of the time that they are spending on their entertainment gadgets with other interesting things, such as engaging more in active sports or arts and crafts. Make a deliberate effort to supply them with alternative materials or equipment that will help them.

You should also encourage them to begin to develop their talents and learn how to make profits from them. This is a better way to get busy. They can spend the same time that they are spending on their games to create saleable items. (More information about how to make profits from our talents is in one of my books, *'Make Profits from Your Talents.'* Details are on the last page).

As said earlier, it's important to read the Bible and worship God after playing certain kinds of games. This will allow God to protect some people in case they've been exposed to their spiritual enemies.

In case the Reader currently have no Bible, it's available Online or through some Ministries. You can also use some of the electronic device that you have to read the Bible online. There are also many free Gospel Music online that you can make good use of. To my young Readers, please take heed to instructions and follow the laws of God. They will improve and save your life. Other sources of exposure to unclean spirits are the loopholes that people have allowed to be created in their lives through their weaknesses. Below are some examples:

## 1. Unforgiveness

Anyone in unforgiveness will be allowing their enemies to have easy access to their lives. Our souls are designed like houses, with doors and windows. Our ears, eyes, mind, and so on, are the spiritual gates. When we study the Scriptures, praise, worship, and pray to God, His Presence is released around us to cleanse and protect our spiritual gates, as well as prevent unclean spirits from further entry, and touching our stuff. But if we are in unforgiveness, or in any other act of flesh, our spiritual gates will be exposed to them because we have temporarily 'lost' God's Presence (our spiritual 'Body Guard'), which is supposed to shield us from unclean spirits. We have indirectly made it easy for them to access the area that they are not supposed to have access to. This is the flesh realm and the Anointing does not dwell there.

*"Therefore if you bring your gift to the altar, and there remember that your brother has something against you,*

*leave your gift there before the altar, and go your way. First be reconciled to your brother, and then come and offer your gift"* Matthew 5:23-24.

The highlighted part of the above Scripture is very important. I want you to meditate on it.

Try all your possible best to make up with people that have offended you, as quickly as you can.

*"Love suffers long and is kind; love does not envy; love does not parade itself, is not puffed up; does not behave rudely, does not seek its own, is not provoked, thinks no evil; does not rejoice in iniquity, but rejoices in the truth; bears all things, believes all things, hopes all things, endures all things"* 1 Corinthians 13:4-7

Please read the whole chapter of 1 Corinthians 13 and take the Scriptures therein seriously. It's important to walk in love.

## 2. Hatred

This is also similar to unforgiveness. If you are the type that has hatred for others, you will be exposing yourself to spiritual enemies. The foundation of the Gospel is based on LOVE. Please take note of this truth: God will make sure that your blessings or breakthroughs for certain things are connected to your loving the people that you hate (as long as your security will not be in jeopardy, if you get close to some of them). Always remember that loving one another is a law in the Kingdom of God.

> *A new commandment I give to you,*
> *that you love one another;*
> *as I have loved you, that you also love one another. By this all will know that you*
> *are My disciples, if you have love for one another"*
> John 13:34-35.

Don't hate if you want your prayers to be answered quickly. I do understand how difficult it is to love some people, especially those who have offended or hurt us greatly or those with ungrateful attitudes. But you can love them because of God, by making sure that you are not in malice with any of them. This is for your own good. Make a deliberate effort to say *'hello'* or pray when your mind is about to go against them.

> *"If it is possible, as much as depends on you, live peaceably with all men"* Romans 12:18.

Use Isaiah 40:29 to pray for spiritual strength:
> *"He gives power to the weak,*
> *And to those who have no might He increases strength."*

## 3. Condemnation

If you are a Christian and are always thinking about your past and feeling guilty, an unclean spirit is trying to create a loophole in your life. This is an attempt to stop what God wants to do in your life, and to prevent you from fulfilling your Divine Assignments.

The Bible says in 2 Corinthians 5:17 that;

> "...If anyone is in Christ, he is a new creation; old things have passed away; behold, all things have become new."

The unclean spirits know that you need faith to do the work of the Gospel and to believe for things in the Kingdom of God. Hence, they will try to make you to walk in condemnation, which will affect your faith.

Once you've asked God for forgiveness and has accepted Jesus Christ as your Lord and Savior, you are not supposed to be thinking about your past because the Blood of Jesus has cleansed you. As said earlier, if you're thinking about your past sins, then you are creating a loop-hole and you lack the deep understanding of what Christianity is all about. God said in Isaiah 43:25 that,

> *""I, even I, am He who blots out your transgressions for My own sake; And I will not remember your sins."*

When the thoughts about your past are coming to your mind, confess and meditate on 2 Corinthians 5:17;

> *"...If anyone is in Christ, he is a new creation; old things have passed away; behold, all things have become new"*

and,

> *"...Forgetting those things which are behind and reaching forward to those things which are ahead, I press toward the goal..."* Philippians 3:13-14.

The Lord knows that traps will be set for some people and has created a way out for us. Once you've accepted Jesus Christ, you are to move on with unwavering faith and not look back at your past.

Don't allow your past mistakes to hold you down if God has instructed you to do some things. Break yourself free with the word of God. Think on the Scripture below for a minute;

> *"You are already clean because of the word which I have spoken to you"* John 15:3.

Take note of this point in the above Scripture; while you are feeling condemned, Jesus Christ said, *"you are already clean."* And if anyone reminds you of your past mistakes and errors, remind them of the Scriptures below:

> *"...If anyone is in Christ, he is a new creation; old things have passed away; behold, all things have become new"*
> 2 Corinthians 5:17

> *"There is therefore now no condemnation to those who are in Christ Jesus..."* Romans 8:1.

Jesus Christ has cleansed us, removed our shame and crowned us with glory. You are a new creature; your old sinful nature has died. All you have to do now is to remain and abide in Him (through your daily devotions-reading, praising, worshipping, and prayers).

Always write Scriptures on index cards and carry them around with you. They are your shield against unwanted thoughts.

> *"The sacrifices of God are a broken spirit,*
> *A broken and a contrite heart—*
> *These, O God, You will not despise"* Psalm 51:17.

(Please search for more relevant Scriptures. See Chapter 5 Guide 'Q').

### 4. Addiction

If you cannot stop yourself from doing certain things that you know are wrong, there is another voice, other than the voice of God, speaking to your mind and making you to want to do them. Each time the enemy succeeds in tempting you and you fall into it, you will become spiritually unclean and loose the strength that is supposed to stop you from doing what you don't want to do.

(Use the guide and Scriptures in Chapter 5 Guide 'G' to strengthen your mind whenever you are tempted).

### 5. Anti-Progress Spirit

If you are always sad while others are celebrating or rejoicing, this will create a loophole for your enemies to come into your life. If you are always rejoicing with others, you will reap a harvest of joy.

> *"Rejoice with those who rejoice, and weep with those who weep"* Romans 12:15.

> *"...Whatever a man sows, that he will also reap"*

Galatians 6:7.

## 6. Envy or Jealousy

If you are envious or jealous of other people's success, this attitude will create a loophole in your life. Instead, pray for such success to flow into your life and ask the Lord for wisdom to be creative with your talents.

The problem with people who are envious or jealous of others is that they do not know their divine assignments in life. You may be more blessed than the person you are jealous of, if you know what you are supposed to do. Always ask God in your prayers about your divine assignment in life. (Please see Chapter 5 Guide 'B' for some tips on hearing clearly from God).

## 7. Sexual Immorality

If you commit any form of sexual sin, you will be exposed to unclean spirits. Always pray for strength if you are weak in this area and don't allow thoughts from your past to have a grip on you. Always remember that the Blood of Jesus has cleansed you when you accepted Him.

(If you are addicted to pornography or any other addictive behavior, please follow the instructions in Chapter 5 Guide 'G').

> *"He gives power to the weak,*
> *And to those who have no might He increases*
> *strength"* Isaiah 40:29.

> *"Flee sexual immorality…"* 1 Corinthians 6:18.

> *"Truly, these times of ignorance God overlooked, but now commands all men everywhere to repent…"* Acts 17:30.

## 8. Anger

If you are the type that is easily offended or bad tempered, you will be exposing yourself to unclean spirits.

> *"Cease from anger, and forsake wrath;*
> *Do not fret—it only causes harm"* Psalm 37:8.

Calmness of the soul is required before the Holy Spirit can effectively work on us. Angry and agitated soul repels Him.

> *"He makes me to lie down in green pastures;*
> *He leads me beside the still waters.*
> *He restores my soul…"* Psalm 23:2-3.

(Use the guide in Chapter 5 Guide 'H' if you need strength in this area of your life).

## 9. Sadness/Depression

This is also one of the major door-way for unclean spirits to enter people's lives. Whenever you start to feel sad, you must do something quickly to replenish your joy. Start by reading some relevant Scriptures (especially Psalms), and praise and worship God. This will drive out the enemy responsible for your sadness, and it will also release the spirit of joy and spiritual strength back into your life. (More information about dealing with sadness and depression in Chapter 5 Guide 'J').

It's important to note that alcohol and drugs provide only temporary joy. They are not the answer to resolve life's problems, but the Joy of the Lord. This Joy is obtainable through reading of the Scriptures, praise and worshipping Him. Also, those engaging in the use of alcohol and drugs need to know that those habits do not improve people's lives but rather make things worse for them. Most of the time, what they are going through are spiritual problems that require spiritual solutions. Only the Joy of the Lord can give people the void-filling Joy that they are searching for, and the strength to keep going in life.

> "...*Do not sorrow, for the joy of the* LORD *is your strength*" **Nehemiah 8:10.**

As mentioned earlier, the above discussed Points are some examples of what can lead to exposure to unclean spirits. We now have emergency situations in the world and God wants to rectify the various unpleasant situations that many people are currently under-going. But the divine solutions will not automatically happen unless those who need divine assistance study the Scriptures, praise, worship and pray fervently, more than their usual practices. The next few chapters will highlight some Divine Solutions.

*"If My people who are called by My name will humble themselves, and pray and seek My face, and turn from their wicked ways, then I will hear from heaven, and will forgive their sin and heal their land"*
2 Chronicles 7:14.

# Chapter Two

## The Power of the Scriptures

*"This Book of the Law shall not depart from your mouth, but you shall meditate in it day and night, that you may observe to do according to all that is written in it. For then you will make your way prosperous, and then you will have good success"* Joshua 1:8.

Christians who are inconsistent with their Bible Study are easy targets for their spiritual enemies. We all know that after a woman has visited the salon, she will look radiant. This can be likened to reading of the Scriptures and praising/worshipping. The enemies of our Souls can differentiate between Christians that have read and those that have not. This is because, those who have read and worshipped will 'glow' in the spirit because of the glory of God that is around them, and those that have not, will appear 'dull and malnourished.'

The Scriptures can be read and applied to any situation through one or more of the following methods:

Reading
Sowing
Memorizing

and Meditating.

Let's now see how each of the above methods of reading the Bible can be used to provide divine solutions to our various situations.

# Reading

*"...I have treasured the words of His mouth
More than my necessary food"*
Job 23:12.

*"I cling to Your testimonies..."* Psalm 119:31.

If you are experiencing some spiritual afflictions and you want a relief or prevent unclean spirits from entering your life, you will need to read several chapters of the Bible at one time and at least twice daily. You must treat the Scriptures as if it's your physical regular meals and read them dedicatedly.

*"I will delight myself in Your statutes;
I will not forget Your word"* Psalm 119:16.

*"...I have treasured the words of His mouth
more than my necessary food"*
Job 23:12.

*"...His delight is in the law of the LORD, And in His law he meditates day and night"* Psalm 1:2.

The Book of Psalms is one of the most powerful Books in the Bible that can be used to release the Anointing for our protection, as well as for the relief of spiritual afflictions. The Book has to be read generously for it to be effective. Reading several chapters at one time can be likened to a situation whereby a coat of paint is applied to a damaged wall. The more chapters that you are able to read will release more of God's Anointing into your life.

Also, any unclean spirit that you are harboring will be driven out (but praise and worship may be required for this to occur). In some sections of the Bible, such as those that are specifically for praising (for examples Psalms 96-99), the anointing can be released without worshipping with music or use of verbal adoration.

Secondly, the effect that is generated after reading several chapters can be likened to a physical weight being placed on an object. Many of the chapters that you are able to read will act as 'spiritual weight', which will prevent your mind from wandering around, as well as prevent unwanted thoughts from being implanted by unseen enemies.

Practice reading fast because the idea is to read several chapters at one time for it to be effective. It's also very important to worship God each time you read the Scriptures. This will allow the Holy Spirit to come and help you. Worshipping creates the pathway for the Spirit of God to come, and to also take us higher to the realm above flesh, where prayers are answered, and breakthroughs occur. (More about Worship in Chapter 3).

I will also advise you to strive to keep sin out of your life because it will hinder the Presence of God from manifesting. Always ask for forgiveness every time you pray, as you never know when and where you may have erred.

# Relevant Scriptures

As said earlier, the Book of Psalms contains important Scriptures that can be used to release the Anointing. I will also suggest that you should make an effort to read Psalm 119 and 136 as often as possible.

Other examples of Scriptures that are useful, especially for those going through spiritual afflictions can be found in the following Scriptures:

The Book of Ezekiel Chapters 40-43
Exodus Chapters 25-28
Acts of the Apostles Chapters 1 & 2
1 Kings Chapters 6-8, and generally where the Bible talks about the Anointing or describes 'The Temple'.

(Use the Self-help pages at the end of this book to record other relevant Scriptures during your Bible Study).

# Saying Scriptures Repeatedly (Sowing)

*"The sower sows the word"* Mark 4:14.

When we say some Scriptures repeatedly, we are sowing them in the spirit (just as farmers sow their seed in their farms physically), and spiritual harvest will follow. Also, it's advantageous to play gospel music or sing after saying the Scriptures. This can be likened to having a drink after eating. (The exception is when we use the Scriptures to rebuke unclean spirits or speak to a situation. But this must be done by faith).

I once asked the Lord why it's important to repeat some Scriptures. This is what He revealed; that just as the walls in a physical building are built by arranging bricks in layers, our spiritual wall is also being built when we say certain Scriptures repeatedly. Sometimes when we are experiencing spiritual attacks, repeating certain Scriptures will create a wall of protection around us. We are permitting God to do what we are commanding, through the Scriptures.

If you are currently going through some spiritual attacks, please do the following; read some Psalms (for example, from 97-100, 145-150), and repeat the Scripture below several times:

*"For I,' says the LORD, 'will be a wall of fire all around her, and I will be the glory in her midst'"* Zechariah 2:5.

Play a praise music that you like immediately after reading. (It's important that you dance while the music is playing). Follow this with worship music and prayers. The worship is required because a void was created during praise, and the void needs to be filled. (Please read Matthew 12:43-45 for more understanding). You will see the profound effect that the above steps will generate.

(There are some Guides listed in Chapter 5 to help with various spiritual situations).

If our spiritual wall is in place, it will be impossible to be exposed to our enemies, but sin or flesh can prevent this from happening. Also, sometimes some acts of flesh or sin can make the wall to become 'damaged'. Sin can also prevent the Scriptures from manifesting its spiritual effects. We must therefore be careful; *"work out your own salvation with fear and trembling"* Philippians 2:12.

There are other Scriptures that can be sown for various spiritual conditions in the Bible. I will encourage you to search for them, compile the ones that are relevant to your situation, and keep a record of them for future use. I will also suggest that the listed Scriptures below or the ones that you will compile should be repeated at least twice daily.

## Relevant Scriptures

*"Instead of the thorn shall come up the cypress tree, and instead of the brier shall come up the myrtle tree"* Isaiah 55:13.

*"…The glory of the LORD went up from the cherub, and paused over the threshold of the temple; and the house was filled with the cloud, and the court was full of the brightness of the LORD's glory"* Ezekiel 10:4.

*"He gives power to the weak, And to those who have no might He increases strength"* Isaiah 40:29.
*"Rejoice the soul of Your servant, For to You, O Lord, I lift up my soul"* Psalm 86:4.

*"Every plant which My heavenly Father has not planted will be uprooted"* Matthew 15:13.
Several verses of Psalm 119 are also good for the purpose discussed above.

(Use the Self-help pages at the end of this book to record some Scriptures during your Bible Study if you do not have Scripture Journal at the moment).

# Meditation

*"This Book of the Law shall not depart from your mouth, but you shall meditate in it day and night…"* Joshua 1:8.

*"You will keep him in perfect peace, Whose mind is stayed on You…"* Isaiah 26:3.

Many Scriptures have hidden spiritual meanings and only the Holy Spirit can reveal them to us. The meanings are imparted intuitively when we meditate on them. This is done when we continuously think on a particular Scripture until the spiritual meaning is imparted into our mind. If you, the Reader have not meditated on Scriptures before, I will encourage you to begin as soon as possible.

The experience can be likened to when we are attempting to cut through a shell that has some honey in the center. When you strike the shell several times, the honey will come out. It's an amazing thing to experience God this way. Always say the Scripture below before meditating:

> "... He opened their understanding, that they might comprehend the Scriptures" Luke 24:45.

**Spiritual Implication:** When the true meaning of a Scripture is intuitively imparted, some strength is also released. This is to strengthen the mind against spiritual attacks (prevention of bad thoughts), and temptations. Also, the mind is simultaneously cleansed from bad thoughts or evil images that may have been implanted by unseen enemies.

One other key advantage of meditation is the impartation of high intelligence. I will suggest that you should meditate on the Book of Proverbs as much as you can (especially Students who are struggling with their studies).

> "I have more understanding than all my teachers,
> For Your testimonies are my meditation"
> Psalm 119:99.

For those with severe cases of afflictions of the mind, meditating on Scriptures with images is the best method of dealing with such situation. Please see some examples below.

# Relevant Scriptures

Some examples of Scriptures with images are in

Exodus 25:10-22, 23-30, 31-40 and 1 King Chapters 6 and 7. You should make an effort to sketch the images and meditate on them daily. Do this by sketching or drawing, looking, and thinking about them several times. Sketch some on an index card (the blank side) and carry them with you as you go about your daily activities. Ask the Holy Spirit some questions while you are meditating on them. When you do this, the images on your mind will gradually be erased.

I will also suggest that you should purchase a sketch pad solely for this divine activity, and search for more Scriptures with images and keep a record of them. If you're gifted in drawing, some of your drawings can be developed into saleable art works.

The next few pages contain some pictures that I drew while I was going through some spiritual afflictions:

## The Lampstand in the Sanctuary.
## (From Hebrews 9:1-2).

*"Then indeed, even the first covenant had ordinances of divine service and the earthly sanctuary. For a tabernacle was prepared: the first part, in which was the lampstand, the table, and the showbread, which is called the sanctuary;"*
Hebrew 9:1-2.

# Aaron
## (From Leviticus 8:6-7).

*"Then Moses brought Aaron and his sons and washed them with water. And he put the tunic on him, girded him with the sash, clothed him with the robe, and put the ephod on him; and he girded him with the intricately woven band of the ephod, and with it tied the ephod on him."*
Leviticus 8:6-7.

## The Mercy Seat
*(From Hebrews 9:5).*

*"...Above it were the cherubim of glory overshadowing the mercy seat. Of these things we cannot now speak in detail"*
**Hebrews 9:5.**

## A Cherub (From Exodus 26:31).

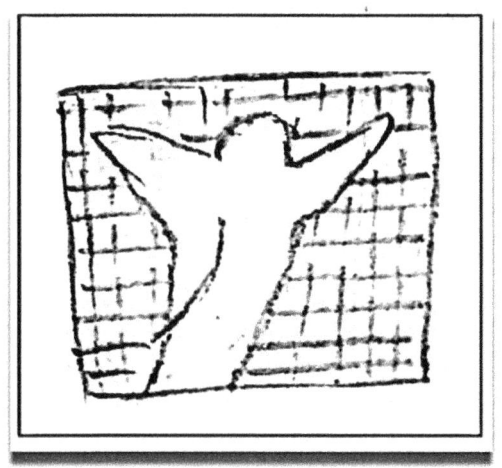

*"You shall make a veil woven of blue, purple, and scarlet thread, and fine woven linen. It shall be woven with an artistic design of cherubim"* Exodus 26:31.

(Use the Self-help pages at the end of this book to record the Scriptures that you'll like to sketch or draw).

## Memorization

*"And these words which I command you today shall be in your heart"* Deuteronomy 6:6.

Memorization of the Scriptures is one of the most powerful weapons for spiritual warfare. It's basically the same as how we used to memorize some numbers in school.

Evil thoughts or images are thorns. When you memorize a Scripture, any evil thought or image that may have been implanted into your mind and are difficult to erase or forget will be uprooted! When a Scripture is memorized, it 'anchors' itself into the mind in order to prevent the implantation of evil images and bad thoughts, as well as uproot the evil thoughts that may have already been implanted.

A good example of a Scripture that can be memorized for this purpose is Isaiah 55:13. If you are going through affliction of the mind, I want you to memorize the Scripture below and see the result for yourself. Try to memorize it by heart several times during the day:

*"Instead of the thorn shall come up the cypress tree, and instead of the brier shall come up the myrtle tree."*

The act of trying to remember the Scripture is what generates the spiritual power. This process keeps the mind clean and protected, and it's also a spiritual brick-wall against the enemies that may be trying to afflict the mind with bad thoughts or evil images.

It's also important to memorize Scriptures in case of other spiritual emergencies. Sometimes we may need to speak to a situation in order to counter an evil attack. We can move mountains through our confessions.

# Relevant Scriptures

*"No weapon formed against you shall prosper…"* Isaiah 54:17.

*"…The righteous are bold as a lion"* Proverbs 28:1.

*"Let God arise, let His enemies be scattered; let those also who hate Him flee before Him. As smoke is driven away, so drive them away; as wax melts before the fire, so let the wicked perish at the presence of God. But let the righteous be glad; let them rejoice before God; yes, let them rejoice exceedingly"* Psalm 68:1-3.

*"He permitted no one to do them wrong; yes, He rebuked kings for their sakes, saying, "Do not touch My anointed ones, and do My prophets no harm"* Psalm 105:14-15.

I will encourage you to attempt some or all the above methods of reading the Scriptures daily. Don't forget to worship God immediately after doing any or all of them. You can also sing if playing music is not convenient or do verbal praise if you do not know any Christian song. Start by praising God for His creations, faithfulness, and so on.

(Use the Self-help pages at the end of this book to record the Scriptures that you'll like to memorize daily. I will advise you to purchase a Scripture Journal as soon as possible).

# Chapter Three

## The Power of Praise & Worship

*"I will bless the Lord at all times;
His praise shall continually be in my mouth"*
Psalm 34:1.

*"I spread out my hands to You;
My soul longs for You like a thirsty land"*
Psalm 143:6.

From the preceding chapter, the Scriptures that you have read, sown, meditated on, or memorized, require some 'spiritual water', which is your worship. That is, as water is to physical foods, so is your worship to the Scriptures that you have read.

One of the reasons why many Christians are not seeing results is because they are not worshipping or singing after reading the Scriptures. It's therefore important to praise and worship God immediately after reading. (As said earlier, the exception is when you are using the Scriptures to rebuke unclean spirits or speaking to a situation. But you must do this by faith).

Let's briefly look at praise and worship separately.

# Praise

Praise is used to entertain and get God's attention. It's during praise that spiritual warfare takes place, the unclean spirits are driven out, breakthroughs are achieved, generational curses are broken, and spiritual hindrances are pulled down. Furthermore, we will become spiritually clean during the dance and ready for divine union with God, which will take place during worship.

> *"Let the high praises of God be in their mouth,*
> *And a two-edged sword in their hand,*
> *To execute vengeance on the nations,*
> *And punishments on the peoples;*
> *To bind their kings with chains,*
> *And their nobles with fetters of iron..."*
> Psalm 149:6-8.

Most of the victories won from spiritual battles by many of the Prophets and Apostles in the Bible were achieved during praise.

> *"But at midnight Paul and Silas were praying and singing hymns to God, and the prisoners were listening to them. Suddenly there was a great earthquake, so that the foundations of the prison were shaken; and immediately all*

*the doors were opened, and everyone's chains were loosed"* Acts 16:25-26.

(For the sake of new Christians, Gospel Praise Music are usually the ones with fast and danceable beats).

# Worship

Worshipping God is an act of honoring, adoring and showing reverence to our Creator. Worship keeps us in a state of purity (because of the Presence released), and to have a closer relationship with God. It's important to make this your daily habit as with praise.

Worship usually follows immediately after praise. This is because, if an unclean spirit was driven out during praise, the void created can be filled with the Anointing during worship. Also, it's during worship that blessings are released, Soul repairs takes place (if there's any spiritual injury). This is God's Clinic!

Furthermore, divine idea(s) are also imparted into some people's lives, which is the reward for 'visiting' and entertaining the King, and for being faithful in the Kingdom of God.

Worshipping can be done either by singing, playing worship music, or by verbal adoration. As mentioned earlier, if we are in a state of spiritual uncleanness, we cannot enter the Presence of God (hence praise is a pre-requisite). It is important that we ask for forgiveness from habitual sins before beginning praise and worship and be prepared for divine union with God.

Let's look briefly at Obadiah 1:17:

> "...On Mount Zion there shall be deliverance,
> And there shall be holiness..."

The above Scripture means that our deliverance can only come from Mount Zion, that is, a higher realm of the spirit, which is attainable during praise and worship. Therefore, if you need to be delivered from any kind of problem, you have to go to *"Mount Zion"*. As said earlier, it's important to strive to keep sin out of your life as this can prevent you from entering God's Presence.

There are days that you will not feel God's Presence when you are worshipping. Don't think that He's not present. He is! Just continue your worship as normal.

(For the sake of new Believers, Gospel Worship Music are usually the ones with softer beats. There are many Praise and Worship Music on YouTube and iTunes to help you).

## Some Helpful Tips About Praise and Worship:

a. If you dance during your praise every day, you will not only get God's attention, but have fewer or no enemies, as well as being blessed beyond what you have asked for! The Scripture below is from King Solomon in the Bible:

> *"...Now the Lord my God has given me rest on every side; there is neither adversary nor evil occurrence"*
> 1 Kings 5:4.

This type of deliverance will require that you do the kind of dance that was done by King David in the Bible on a daily basis:

> *"...David danced before the LORD with all his might"* 2 Samuel 6:14.

b. For super high praise, use a pair of headphones and stay in a secluded area
c. Your praise and worship will become more powerful if you read certain Scriptures prior to praising and worshipping God.

Below are some examples of Scriptures for praise and worship.

# Relevant Scriptures

In order not to interrupt your worship, you should read all the Scriptures before praise. You can repeat them as many times as you like:

> *"Let the high praises of God be in their mouth,*
> *And a two-edged sword in their hand"*
> **Psalm 149:6.**

> *"Rejoice the soul of Your servant,*
> *For to You, O Lord, I lift up my soul"*
> **Psalm 86:4.**

> *"Let the peoples praise You, O God;*
> *Let all the peoples praise You...."*
> **Psalm 67:5-6.**

> *"The LORD reigns, He is clothed with majesty;*
> *The LORD is clothed,*
> *He has girded Himself with strength"*
> **Psalm 93:1.**

> *"Lift up your heads, O you gates!*
> *And be lifted up, you everlasting doors!*
> *And the King of glory shall come in.*
> *Who is this King of glory?*
> *The LORD strong and mighty,*
> *The LORD mighty in battle.*
> *Lift up your heads, O you gates!*

*Lift up, you everlasting doors!*
*And the King of glory shall come in.*
*Who is this King of glory?*
*The* L̲O̲R̲D̲ *of hosts,*
*He is the King of glory"* Psalm 24:7-10.

*"As the deer pants for the water brooks, So pants my soul for You, O God. My soul thirsts for God, for the living God. When shall I come and appear before God?"*
Psalm 42:1-2.

*"O God, You are my God; Early will I seek You; My soul thirsts for You; My flesh longs for You In a dry and thirsty land where there is no water"* Psalm 63:1.

*"How lovely is Your tabernacle, O* L̲O̲R̲D̲ *of hosts! My soul longs, yes, even faints for the courts of the* L̲O̲R̲D̲*; My heart and my flesh cry out for the living God"*
Psalm 84:1-2.

*"...The ransomed of the* L̲O̲R̲D̲ *shall return, and come to Zion with singing, With everlasting joy on their heads. They shall obtain joy and gladness,*
*And sorrow and sighing shall flee away"*
Isaiah 35:10.

*"He opened the rock, and water gushed out;*
*It ran in the dry places like a river"*
Psalm 105:41.

> "...*On Mount Zion there shall be deliverance,
> And there shall be holiness...*" Obadiah 1:17.

You are not limited to only the listed Scriptures. Search for other relevant ones during your Bible Study. You can also read any of the Psalms that the content is about praising the LORD or God. For example, Psalms 97, 98, 146-150.

# Chapter Four

# The Importance of God's Presence

*"For I,' says the LORD, 'will be a wall of fire all around her, and I will be the glory in her midst'"*
Zechariah 2:5.

As mentioned in Chapter One, the increased problems and many unpleasant situations around us now demand that we seek God's Presence more than our usual methods. After we have invited Jesus Christ into our lives, and we begin to read the Scriptures, praise, worship, and pray to God (as well as strive to keep sin at bay), His Presence will come, cleanse and protect us from our enemies, as well as acts as our 'Body Guard'. This is to prevent further entry from unclean spirits.

As said earlier, just as physical buildings have doors and windows, we are also created with doors and windows. Our ears, eyes, and mind are gates, and the same with our Soul. When we read the Scriptures and worship God, His Presence surrounds us and takes its place at our spiritual gates. But some things can make the Presence to leave momentarily. For example, when we are in any act of flesh or have sinned, His Presence will leave but return after we have repented and begin to study the Word, praise, worship or adore God again.

Let's look at the example of King David and King Saul in 1 Samuel Chapter 16. Whenever King David played his musical instrument, the harp, the Presence of God comes and displaces the distressing spirit that was troubling King Saul.

1 Samuel 16 Verses 14-16 says,

> "But the Spirit of the LORD departed from Saul, and a distressing spirit from the LORD troubled him. And Saul's servants said to him, "Surely, a distressing spirit from God is troubling you. Let our master now command your servants, who are before you, to seek out a man who is a skillful player on the harp. And it shall be that he will play it with his hand when the distressing spirit from God is upon you, and you shall be well."

Verse 23 says,

> "And so it was, whenever the spirit from God was upon Saul, that David would take a harp and play it with his hand. Then Saul would become refreshed and well, and the distressing spirit would depart from him."

It's important to note in the above Scriptures the powerful effect that God's Presence had on King Saul.

God's Presence is our spiritual protection and everything that belong to us. We are to strive to enter in, daily. His Presence will also ease our spiritual pain when we are afflicted. It's therefore mandatory that we read the Scriptures, praise, worship and pray intensively, every day, if we want God to help us.

## Relevant Scriptures

*"This Book of the Law shall not depart from your mouth, but you shall meditate in it day and night, that you may observe to do according to all that is written in it..."* Joshua 1:8.

*"Great peace have those who love Your law,
And nothing causes them to stumble"*
Psalm 119:165.

*"You will keep him in perfect peace whose mind is stayed on You..."* Isaiah 26:3.

# Chapter Five

## *Divine Guides for Handling Some Life Situations*

**IMPORTANT!**

If you have not accepted Jesus Christ as your Lord and Savior, please say the prayer below. This is because you need the help of the Holy Spirit. The Spirit of God does everything!

*Dear Heavenly Father, please forgive me of my sins. I now accept Jesus Christ as my Lord and Savior. Let Your Holy Spirit come and help me and reveal my divine purpose to me. In Jesus Name, Amen.*

It's important that you read the Scriptures, praise, worship, and pray every day, as well as go to church and serve God. It's important to observe your Bible Study time consistently (twice daily is better). And if your status or situation does not permit you to attend church services at the moment, you can start one in your house or find a good Online Church. Pray for guide to a good church.

*"...Where two or three are gathered together in My name, I am there in the midst of them"* Matthew 18:20.

(More information about knowing God further @ christytolaministries.org/importantinfo.html.

*" Come to Me, all you who labor and are heavy laden, and I will give you rest"* Matthew 11:28.

*"...I will sprinkle clean water on you, and you shall be clean; I will cleanse you from all your filthiness and from all your idols"* Ezekiel 36:25.

*"It shall come to pass in that day
That his burden will be taken away from your shoulder,
And his yoke from your neck,
And the yoke will be destroyed because of the anointing oil"*
Isaiah 10:27.

    God has equipped us with all the necessary tools that will aid our deliverance. This is because we have the Scriptures and various Gospel Praise and Worship Music at our disposal. There is now the need for us to make good use of them in order to draw God's Mighty Power to our various situations.

    Gospel Praise and Worship Music are designed for various spiritual situations. Some are for adoring, praising or worshipping God. Others are for deliverance, healing, calling of Angels and so on. There are also various Scriptures that can be used to create more powerful effect of the Anointing, when we are praising and worshipping God, as described in chapter three.

Because of the Divine Orders of Things in the Kingdom of God, there is the need for us to know how to appropriately apply the right Music and Scriptures to our situations. For example, if a church service is about deliverance, dancing is important and most of the music should be danceable praise music. Also, the lyrics should express the mightiness of God, or His praises expressed in similar ways. Therefore, there's the need for Christians to know the different functions of the different gospel music that are available, and to also use them to meet their various spiritual needs appropriately. Attention must always be paid to the contents of the lyrics.

The instructions given below will help you to meet some of your spiritual needs. They are designed to help in moments of doubt or when you are in need of urgent spiritual assistance, and you don't know what to do.

In Christianity, a simple prayer of faith with daily and consistent Bible Study and Praise/Worship, are what we required in resolving most of our difficult life situations. But the Bible also says that, *"...Faith by itself, if it does not have works, is dead"* (James 2:17). That is, there will be some instances that some actions will be required in addition to a simple prayer of faith. Hence, the Guides listed below are designed to help you in dealing with some areas of your life that may appear difficult and defying your faith. Many of the Guides will also bring joy into your life.

Once again, it's important to strive to keep sin out of your life. Before attempting any of them, ask God to forgive you of your sins, as you don't know where you may have erred, and the Holy Spirit is grieved. Sin will hinder you from entering God's Presence and prevent Him from helping you. You must also learn to forgive people quickly.

Try as much as possible to repeat the Guide that is suitable for your situation twice daily and write relevant Scriptures on index cards for meditation during the day. I will also encourage you to always dance anytime you are playing melodious tunes to the Lord. This moves the hand of God very quickly.

Please note: The Book of Psalms and any other chapter(s) that you will read at the beginning of each Guide are to serve as the base Scriptures to help generate the spiritual strength that you will require, before praise and worship.

## A. For Those Seeking to Enter God's Presence

1. Read five or more Chapters of the Book of Psalms, especially the ones that are about praising God (for example Psalm 146-150)
2. Read 1 Kings 7 and Ezekiel 1
3. Please say the following Scriptures:

> *"Lift up your heads, O you gates!*
> *And be lifted up, you everlasting doors!*
> *And the King of glory shall come in.*
> *Who is this King of glory?*
> *The LORD strong and mighty,*
> *The LORD mighty in battle.*
> *Lift up your heads, O you gates!*
> *Lift up, you everlasting doors!*
> *And the King of glory shall come in.*
> *Who is this King of glory?*
> *The LORD of hosts,*
> *He is the King of glory"* **Psalm 24:7-10.**

*"O God, You are my God; Early will I seek You; My soul thirsts for You; My flesh longs for You In a dry and thirsty land where there is no water"*
**Psalm 63:1.**

*"One thing I have desired of the LORD, That will I seek: That I may dwell in the house of the LORD all the days of my life,*

> *To behold the beauty of the* LORD,
> *And to inquire in His temple"* Psalm 27:4.

> *"As the deer pants for the water brooks,*
> *So pants my soul for You, O God. My soul thirsts*
> *for God, for the living God. When shall I come*
> *and appear before God?"* Psalm 42:1-2.

4. Dance to your favorite gospel praise music followed by worship music or sing some songs of adoration to God (You can do verbal praise if you do not have access to gospel music or know any gospel song)
5. Pray as you desire.

## B. Hearing Clearly from God

1. Read some Chapters of the Book of Psalms
2. Read 1 Samuel 3:1-10 and John 10:3-5
3. Please say the following Scriptures:

> *"In all your ways acknowledge Him,*
> *And He shall direct your paths"*
> Proverbs 3:6.

> *"I will instruct you and teach you in the way you*
> *should go; I will guide you with My eye"*
> Psalm 32:8.

> *"My soul wait silently for God alone,*
> *For my expectation is from Him"* Psalm 62:5.
> *"Oh, send out Your light and Your truth!*
> *Let them lead me..."* Psalm 43:3.

4. Worship God with your favorite gospel music or sing songs of adoration to Him (I will recommend 'God is Here' by Martha Munizzi on YouTube. The Lyrics goes with your prayer request)
5. Pray as you are led
6. Ask God your questions.

Try your best to exercise your faith and have a heart of expectation to hear from God.

**Important**:
Always keep a notepad and pen with you and write down the instructions you'll receive from God. He can speak when you least expected and in any form that He chooses-dream, vision, intuition or verbal. He can also send someone to give you instructions. You must act on the divine instruction that you will receive immediately.

Also, try to avoid over-eating, especially when it's close to your bedtime. If you're use to eating before your bedtime, substitute food with fruits. Try your best to prevent flesh from interfering with your spiritual life.

In addition to the above, you'll need to continuously listen to Psalms, praise and worship music on audio, to maintain the atmosphere of God's Presence around you. You can also sing if you have no access to media players.

## C. Divine Guides to Help Those in the Occult

Jesus Christ has paid the ultimate price for all rituals or occult practices. There's no need to participate or rely on any spiritualist or become a member of a secret society for protection. There's a HIGHER POWER that is more than enough to protect you, if you know what to do.

Please follow the instructions below:

1. Read five or more Chapters of the Book of Psalms (the more chapters, the better)
2. Read Hebrews 10, Exodus 37:6-24 and 1 King 7:23-26
3. Please say the following Scriptures as many times as you like:

> *"O God, You are my God;*
> *Early will I seek You;*
> *My soul thirsts for You;*
> *My flesh longs for You*
> *In a dry and thirsty land*
> *Where there is no water" Psalm63:1.*

"...The glory of the L ORD went up from the cherub, and stood over the threshold of the house; and the house was filled with the cloud, and the court was full of the brightness of the L ORD 's glory" **Ezekiel 10:4.**

"I will set nothing wicked before my eyes;
I hate the work of those who fall away;
It shall not cling to me" Psalm 101:3.

A perverse heart shall depart from me;
I will not know wickedness" Psalm 101:4

"Do not incline my heart to any evil thing,
To practice wicked works
With men who work iniquity;
And do not let me eat of their delicacies"
Psalm 141:4

"For the scepter of wickedness shall not rest
On the land allotted to the righteous,
Lest the righteous reach out their hands to iniquity"
Psalm 125:3.

"As the deer pants for the water brooks,
So pants my soul for You, O God.
My soul thirsts for God, for the living God.
When shall I come and appear before God?"
Psalm 42:1-2.

4. (a). Sing or play your favorite praise music that will allow you to dance very well. It's important that you dance as this will set the stage for the Lord to fight your enemies and drive out the unclean spirits.

   (b). Play your favorite worship music immediately after praise, as this will draw the Holy Spirit quicker to you, to fill the void created during worship (when the unclean spirits were driven out), and place a protective shield around you.

5. Pray and ask for God's help

**For New Christians:** Search for Praise and Worship Music on YouTube or iTunes.

Repeat the above Guide twice daily and do this consistently. Write one or two of the Scripture verses on an index card and meditate on it (or them) during the day.

If you start to experience increased spiritual afflictions, you should also increase reading of the Psalms and listening to gospel music during the day. You are experiencing retaliation because you are about to be delivered from your enemies. You should 'fight' back with the Word and praise and Worship.

Also, play Psalms on Audio at bed-time, and set your Player to 'repeat' so it can play throughout the night. Get a good pair of headphones and continuously listen to Bible on audio and worship music as much as you can, during the day.

If you have none of the above, set your alarm to wake you up to pray during the night.

The instructions on Guide 'N' will also help you against mind control.

It's important to pray for your close relatives against spiritual retaliation.

## D. Overcoming Suicidal Thoughts

If your thoughts are always negative and it's about harming yourself, there may be something special about your life (your missions), and you are very important to God. Your enemies know this, which could be the reason for your afflictions. You must find out who you are (Guide B). Always ask about your divine purpose in your prayers.

If you are feeling spiritually weak, ask God to forgive your habitual sin and say the Scripture below several times before following the Guide:

*"He gives power to the weak,
And to those who have no might He increases strength"*
Isaiah 40:29.

1. Read five or more Chapters of the Book of Psalms
2. Read 1 Chronicles 4:10 and 1 Samuel 16:14
3. Then say the Scriptures below:

*"Deliver those who are drawn toward death,
And hold back those stumbling to the slaughter"*
Proverbs 24:11.

*"…According to the greatness of Your power
Preserve those who are appointed to die"* Psalm 79:11.

*"I shall not die, but live,
And declare the works of the LORD"*
Psalm *118:17.*

*"You will keep him in perfect peace,
Whose mind is stayed on You…"* Isaiah 26:3.

*"The LORD will pass over the door and not allow the
destroyer to come into your houses to strike you"*
Exodus 12:23.

4. Dance to your favorite praise music followed by a good worship music or sing songs of adoration to God (if you have no access to gospel music)

Repeat the praise music if the zeal for dancing did not come the first time (Search for Praise and Worship Music on YouTube if you're a new Believer)

5. Use 1 Chronicles 4:10 to pray fervently immediately after praise and worship

    Ask God to reveal your divine purpose to you. Write down any divine information that you will receive and do them as soon as you can.

I will also suggest that you should listen to Psalms on Audio and gospel music continuously. Also, meditate on the Scriptures and write some on index cards and carry them around during the day to help occupy and strengthen your mind (See also Guide 'N' for sample Scriptures for meditation). Try and maintain a consistent Bible Study and pray as often as possible.

## E. Spiritual Cleansing

(This is good for those who need to read some Scriptures and worship after exposure to spiritually unclean things or have played certain types of games, such as violent or ritual-based games. Before attempting the Guide, ask God to forgive you of your sins, just in case you've involved yourself in abominable things such as rituals).

1. Read five or more Chapters of the Book of Psalms
2. Read 1 Kings 7:23-26
3. Please say the following Scriptures several times:

*"...I will sprinkle clean water on you, and you shall be clean; I will cleanse you from all your filthiness and from all your idols"* Ezekiel 36:25.

*"...The tabernacle shall be sanctified by My glory"* Exodus 29:43.

*"...The glory of the LORD went up from the cherub, and paused over the threshold of the temple; and the house was filled with the cloud, and the court was full of the brightness of the LORD's glory"* Ezekiel 10:4.

*"Instead of the thorn shall come up the cypress tree, and instead of the brier shall come up the myrtle tree"* Isaiah 55:13.

"For the scepter of wickedness shall not rest
On the land allotted to the righteous
Lest the righteous reach out their hands to iniquity" Psalm 125:3.

"Pull me out of the net which they have secretly laid for me,
For You are my strength" Psalm 31:4.

> *"Uphold my steps in Your paths,*
> *That my footsteps may not slip"* Psalm 17:5.

> *"As the deer pants for the water brooks, So pants my soul for You, O God. My soul thirsts for God, for the living God. When shall I come and appear before God?"*
> Psalm 42:1-2.

4. Dance to a praise music followed by your favorite worship music or sing songs of adoration to God. (You can also do verbal praise if you do not know any Christian song)

5. Pray as you are led.

Also, pray for strength to desist from things that defiles and engage more in creative and productive things, such as arts and crafts, or other recreational activities.

## F. If You Are Having Nightmares

(If you are in unforgiveness or are hateful towards people, you will be exposed to unclean spirits and this may be what is responsible for your nightmares. If you have children or close relatives living with you, always pray for them because your enemies can afflict them as a way of retaliating after your deliverance).

1. Read many Chapters of the Book of Psalms (include Psalms 91 and 121)
2. Read Exodus 37:6-9 and 17-24
3. Then say the following Scriptures:

> *"...The Lord will pass over the door and not allow the destroyer to come into your houses to strike you"* Exodus 12:23.

> *"...The glory of the LORD went up from the cherub, and paused over the threshold of the temple; and the house was filled with the cloud, and the court was full of the brightness of the LORD's glory"* Ezekiel 10:4.

> *"I will both lie down in peace, and sleep; For You alone, O LORD, make me dwell in safety"* Psalm 4:8.

> *"For I,' says the LORD, 'will be a wall of fire all around her, and I will be the glory in her midst'"* Zechariah 2:5.

> *"...The glory of the LORD went up from the cherub, and stood over the threshold of the house; and the house was filled with the cloud, and the court was full of the brightness of the LORD's glory"* Ezekiel 10:4.

4. Dance to your favorite praise music followed by worship music or sing songs of adoration to God. (You can also do verbal praise if you do not know any Christian song.

5. Pray as you are led.

It's important to listen to the Book of Psalms on Audio, and other Scriptures and worship music at bedtime. Set the audio to play throughout the night. There are many gospel music on YouTube/iTunes for your use.

Also, set an alarm to wake you up to pray during the night. Ask the Lord to reveal the root cause of your problems in your prayers if the afflictions persist.

## G. If You Are Struggling with Addictions

(Dancing is important here because this is where the Lord drives out the unclean spirit).

1. Read five or more Chapters of the Book of Psalms
2. Read Acts 2:1-2 and 1 Kings 7:27-37
3. Please say the following Scriptures:

> *"As the deer pants for the water brooks,*
> *So pants my soul for You, O God.*
> *My soul thirsts for God, for the living God.*
> *When shall I come and appear before God?"*

Psalm 42:1-2.

*"...The glory of the LORD went up from the cherub, and stood over the threshold of the house; and the house was filled with the cloud, and the court was full of the brightness of the LORD's glory"* **Ezekiel 10:4.**

*"...They will by no means follow a stranger, but will flee from him, for they do not know the voice of strangers"* **John 10:15.**

*"That He would grant you, according to the riches of His glory, to be strengthened with might through His Spirit in the inner man"* **Ephesians 3:16.**

*"...I will walk at liberty, For I seek Your precepts"* **Psalm 119:45.**

4. Dance to a praise music (repeat the praise music if the zeal for dancing did not come the first time)
5. Play your favorite worship music immediately after praise or sing songs of adoration to God. (You can also do verbal praise if you do not know any Christian song. Pray with the above Scriptures and search for more relevant ones

Listen to Psalms and praise and worship music to maintain God's Presence around you all the time. A pair of good headphones is an advantage.

Read the Psalms and sing all the time if you have no access to the audio version. Write some Scriptures on a piece of paper or index card and take with you during the day for meditation.

## H. Managing Anger Spiritually

1. Read five or more Chapters of the Book of Psalms
2. Read Psalm 23:2-3 (Confess the Scripture to yourself)
3. Say the following Scriptures:

*"Cease from anger and forsake wrath..."* Psalm 37:8.

*"He gives power to the weak
And to those who have no might
He increases strength."* Isaiah 40:29.

*"Uphold my steps in Your paths,
That my footsteps may not slip"* Psalm 17:5.

4. Dance to a good gospel music to worship/adore God
5. Pray for strength and say Psalm 17:5 (below) repeatedly when you are about to lose your temper.

*"Uphold my steps in Your paths,
That my footsteps may not slip"*

(It's important for you to memorize the above Scripture).

Please follow the instructions above twice daily and listen to Psalms on audio, praise and worship music to maintain God's Presence around you until your situation is under control.

Read the Psalms generously, sing, and pray all the time if you have no access to the audio version of the Book of Psalm.

It's also important that you develop a consistent devotional time daily. This will allow God to fill you with His Anointing, which will give you the extra strength that you require.

## I. If You Are Feeling Unwell

(**Important:** The instructions given below are for taking care of the spiritual aspects of your condition/situation. Please do not stop taking your medications or treatments).

1. Read five or more Chapters of the Book of Psalms
2. Read Luke 4:38-40
3. Please say the following Scriptures:

> *"But if the Spirit of Him who raised Jesus from the dead dwells in you, He who raised Christ from the dead will also give life to your mortal bodies through His Spirit who dwells in you"* Romans 8:11.
>
> *"By His stripes we are healed"* Isaiah 53:5.
>
> *"...He Himself took our infirmities and bore our sicknesses"* Matthew 8:17.
>
> *"I shall not die, but live and declare the works of the LORD"* Psalm 118: 17.
>
> *"...O dry bones, hear the word of the LORD! Thus says the Lord GOD to these bones: "Surely I will cause breath to enter into you, and you shall live. I will put sinews on you and bring flesh upon you, cover you with skin and put breath in you; and you shall live"* Ezekiel 37:4-6.
>
> *"...If you diligently heed the voice of the LORD your God and do what is right in His sight, give ear to His commandments and keep all His statutes, I will put none of the diseases on you which I have brought on the Egyptians. For I am the LORD who heals you"* Exodus 15:26.

4. Play any healing gospel music or sing songs that the lyrics are about healing
5. Pray as you desire.

(In case you are a new Christian, there are many Gospel Healing Music on YouTube/iTunes).

## J. If You Are Sad or Depressed

(Dancing is important here because this is where the Lord will drive out the unclean spirit that is responsible for your sadness/depression).

1. Read five or more Chapters of the Book of Psalms
2. Read 1 Samuel 16:14-23.
3. Then say the following Scriptures repeatedly:

> *"He gives power to the weak, And to those who have no might He increases strength"* Isaiah 40:29.

> *"Rejoice the soul of Your servant, For to You, O Lord, I lift up my soul"* Psalm 86:4.

> *"Rejoice in the Lord always. Again I will say, rejoice!"* Philippians 4:4.

> *"...The joy of the* LORD *is your strength"* Nehemiah 8:10.

> *"As the deer pants for the water brooks,*

> *So pants my soul for You, O God.*
> *My soul thirsts for God, for the living God.*
> *When shall I come and appear before God?"*
> Psalm 42:1-2.

> *"Lift up your heads, O you gates!*
> *And be lifted up, you everlasting doors!*
> *And the King of glory shall come in.*
> *Who is this King of glory?*
> *The LORD strong and mighty,*
> *The LORD mighty in battle.*
> *Lift up your heads, O you gates!*
> *Lift up, you everlasting doors!*
> *And the King of glory shall come in.*
> *Who is this King of glory?*
> *The LORD of hosts,*
> *He is the King of glory"* Psalm 24:7-10.

4. Dance to a powerful praise music (the type that will make you to dance with all your strength, like King David in 2 Samuel 6:14), followed by your favorite worship music or sing songs of adoration to God. (I will suggest that you play the praise music twice if the zeal for dancing did not come the first time).
5. Pray as you desire.

## K. For Those with Violence Tendencies

(Dancing is important here)

1. Read five or more Chapters of the Book of Psalms
2. Read Luke 4:31-37, 40-41.
3. Please say the Scriptures below:

*"A perverse heart shall depart from me; I will not know wickedness"* **Psalm 101:4.**

*"… You would keep me from evil, that I may not cause pain!" So God granted him what he requested"*
1 Chronicles 4:10.

*"Do not incline my heart to any evil thing,
To practice wicked works
With men who work iniquity;
And do not let me eat of their delicacies"*
Psalm 141:4.

4. Play and dance to a praise music that will make you to dance very well, and worship God with your favorite gospel music, or sing songs of adoration to Him (there are many on YouTube/iTunes)
5. Pray with the above Scriptures

Continue to listen to the Scriptures on audio and read the Book of Psalm, as well as praising and worshipping daily. This will help to maintain the atmosphere of God's Presence around you. Use a pair of headphones for better result. You can give a verbal praise, if you have no access to gospel music.

## L. For Those Living in Fear or Worried

1. Read five or more Chapters of the Book of Psalms (include Psalm 91 and 121).
2. Read Matthew 11:28-30 and meditate on them
3. Please say the following Scriptures

> *"He makes me to lie down in green pastures;*
> *He leads me beside the still waters.*
> *He restores my soul"* **Psalm 23:2-3.**

> *"For He shall give His angels charge over you,*
> *To keep you in all your ways"* **Psalm 91:11.**

*"For God has not given us a spirit of fear, but of power and of love and of a sound mind"* **2 Timothy 1:7.**

> *"He permitted no one to do them wrong;*
> *Yes, He rebuked kings for their sakes,*
> *Saying, "Do not touch My anointed ones,*
> *And do My prophets no harm"* **Psalm 105:14-15.**

*"The angel of the LORD encamps all*

> *around those who fear Him,*
> *And delivers them"* Psalm 34:7.

> *"Peace I leave with you, My peace I give to you; not as the world gives do I give to you. Let not your heart be troubled, neither let it be afraid"* John 14:27.

4. Praise and worship God with your favorite gospel music or sing songs of adoration to Him. You can do verbal praise if you do not know any Christian gospel music
5. Pray as you desire and use the Scriptures to pray.

I will also suggest that you should read the Psalms and worship more because the Anointing restores confidence. Get a good pair of headphones for better result.

## M. For Those Wrongfully Convicted

1. Read five or more Chapters of the Book of Psalms
2. Read Acts 12:1-17
3. Please say with the following Scriptures:

> *"To You, O LORD, I lift up my soul.*
> *O my God, I trust in You;*
> *Let me not be ashamed;*
> *Let not my enemies triumph over me.*

*Indeed, let no one who waits on You be ashamed…"*
**Psalm 25:1-3.**

*"Vindicate me, O* LORD*,
For I have walked in my integrity.
I have also trusted in the* LORD*;
I shall not slip"* **Psalm 26:1.**

*"To You I will cry, O* LORD *my Rock:
Do not be silent to me,
Lest, if You are silent to me,
I become like those who go down to the pit"*
**Psalm 28:1.**

*"Let the groaning of the prisoner come before You"*
**Psalm 79:11.**

*"I will lift up my eyes to the hills —
From whence comes my help?
My help comes from the* LORD*,
Who made heaven and earth"* **Psalm 121:1.**

*"Unto You I lift up my eyes,
O You who dwell in the heavens.
Behold, as the eyes of servants look to the hand of their masters,
As the eyes of a maid to the hand of her mistress,
So our eyes look to the* LORD *our God,*

*Until He has mercy on us. Have mercy on us, O LORD, have mercy on us!"* Psalm 123:1-3.

4. Praise and worship God with your favorite gospel music or sing songs of adoration to Him. You can do verbal praise if you have no access to gospel music
5. Use Psalm 20 to pray.

## N. If Your Mind is Constantly Attacked

1. Read five or more Chapters of the Book of Psalms and any other Book of your choice
2. Say this Scripture repeatedly;

*"...We have the mind of Christ"* 1 Corinthians 2:16.

3. Please do the following:

Sketch the images in (i) or (ii) below and meditate on them. Please spend some quality time doing this.

It's important that you purchase a sketch pad solely devoted for this purpose, and continue to meditate on them as much as time permits you during the day:

i. *"He also made the lampstand of pure gold; of hammered work he made the lampstand. Its shaft, its branches, its bowls, its ornamental knobs, and its flowers were of the same piece. And six branches came out of its sides: three branches of the lampstand out of one side, and three branches of the lampstand out of the other side. There were three bowls made like almond blossoms on one branch, with an ornamental knob and a flower, and three bowls made like almond blossoms on the other branch, with an ornamental knob and a flower—and so for the six branches coming out of the lampstand.*
*And on the lampstand itself were four bowls made like almond blossoms, each with its ornamental knob and flower. There was a knob under the first two branches of the same, a knob under the second two branches of the same, and a knob under the third two branches of the same, according to the six branches extending from it. Their knobs and their branches were of one piece; all of it was one hammered piece of pure gold"*
Exodus 37:17-22.

ii. *"Moreover the king made a great throne of ivory, and overlaid it with pure gold. The throne had six steps, with a footstool of gold, which were fastened to the throne; there were armrests on either side of the place of the seat, and two lions stood beside the* armrests. Twelve lions stood there, one on each side of the six steps..." 2 Chronicles 9:17-19.

4. Please say the Scriptures below:

*"You will keep him in perfect peace,
Whose mind is stayed on You..."* Isaiah 26:3.

*"...We have the mind of Christ"* 1 Corinthians 2:16.
*"For the scepter of wickedness shall not rest
On the land allotted to the righteous
Lest the righteous reach out their hands to iniquity"*
Psalm 125:3.

*"Inside the inner sanctuary he made two cherubim of olive wood, each ten cubits high"* 1 Kings 6:23.

*"Lift up your heads, O you gates!
And be lifted up, you everlasting doors!
And the King of glory shall come in.
Who is this King of glory?
The LORD strong and mighty,
The LORD mighty in battle.
Lift up your heads, O you gates!
Lift up, you everlasting doors!
And the King of glory shall come in.
Who is this King of glory?*

> *The LORD of hosts,*
> *He is the King of glory"* Psalm 24:7-10.

5. Worship God with your favorite gospel music or sing songs of adoration to Him. You can also do verbal praise if gospel music is not available. (I will encourage you to always dance anytime you are playing melodious tunes to the Lord).
6. Pray as you are led.

Please Note: Your situation will drastically improve if you do this every day and consistently.

Other good examples of Scriptures with images can be found in 1 Kings 7 and 8. Please search for other relevant ones to add to the above. They will surely enrich your life. Always ask the Holy Spirit questions as you sketch the images.

Please listen to the audio versions of the Scriptures and worship music all the time. This will help to maintain the atmosphere of God's Presence around you. Headphones are treasures!

Practice writing Scriptures on index cards for meditation at regular intervals. This will also help to protect your mind. These are your weapons of warfare.

Occupy yourself with developing your God-given talents or other interesting activities. Practice journaling all the time.

## O. For the Unemployed

1. Read five or more Chapters of the Book of Psalms
2. Read 2 Thessalonians 3:7-12 (Petition the Lord with Verse 10)
3. Please say the following Scriptures:

*"Six days you shall labor and do all your work"*
Exodus 20:9.

*"Man goes out to his work, And to his labor until the evening"* Psalm 104:23.
*"...If anyone will not work, neither shall he eat"*
2 Thessalonians 3:10.

*"And Jabez called on the God of Israel saying, "Oh, that You would bless me indeed, and enlarge my territory..."*
1 Chronicles 4:10.

4. Worship God with your favorite gospel music or sing songs of adoration to Him.
5. Pray as you are led
6. Make a special offering or a vow in your church towards this area of need.

Also, find out what your God-given talents are and start to use them. They are given to you so you can make a living out of at least one of them, (in case you have more than one talent).

(You can read more about this in one of my books; *'Profit from Your Talents'*. It's available at amazon.com and other leading bookstores.

## P. Business Owners

1. Read five or more Chapters of the Book of Psalms
2. Read Deuteronomy 28:1-13 (select the Verses that are relevant)
3. Worship God with your favorite gospel music
4. Pray for your business/company with the following Scriptures:

   *"In all labor there is profit..."* Proverbs 14:23.

   *"...Hezekiah prospered in all his works"*
   1 Chronicles 32:30.

   *"...Israel shall blossom and bud,
   And fill the face of the world with fruit"* Isaiah 27:6.

   *"...Please give me success this day..."* Genesis 24:12.

## Q. To Prevent Condemnation

1. Read five or more Chapters of the Book of Psalms
2. Read Romans 8:1-3 (repeat and meditate)
3. Please say the following Scriptures:

*"...If anyone is in Christ, he is a new creation; old things have passed away; behold, all things have become new"* 2 Corinthians 5:17.

*"...Forgetting those things which are behind and reaching forward to those things which are ahead, I press toward the goal for the prize of the upward call of God in Christ Jesus"* Philippians 3:13-14.

*"The sacrifices of God are a broken spirit,*
*A broken and a contrite heart—*
*These, O God, You will not despise"* Psalm 51:17.

*"You are already clean because of the word which I have spoken to you.* John 15:3.

4. Praise and worship God with your favorite gospel music
5. Pray as you are led.

Write some Scriptures on index cards and carry them around with you. They are your shield against unwanted thoughts. See also guide 'N' above if your mind is seriously disturbed about this.

## Spiritual Maintenance

Just as we maintain our physical equipment, it's also important to maintain our spiritual life in order to keep it in a state of spiritual wellness. As earlier said, daily reading of the Scriptures, praising, worshipping, and praying to God, as well as listening to audio versions of the Scriptures, are important in achieving this.

Below are some Website links of some prepared Scriptures for your spiritual maintenance. It's important to play gospel music after listening.

www.christytolaministries.org/ssm.html
www. christytolaministries.org/healing.html
www. christytolaministries.org/nightseed.html
www. christytolaministries.org/spiritualwarfare.html
www. christytolaministries.org/worshipseed.html

Please note that you are not limited to the above prepared audios only. You can combine Scriptures and worship music and tailor them to your needs.

For new Christians; if you have no Bible, you can read Scriptures online. Here are some examples of some Bible Websites:

bible.com
youversion.com
biblegateway.com.

# Chapter Six

## *Conclusion*

God created the Earth that we live in and gave us the Bible as our daily 'Survival Guide'. It's therefore important for us to read it in order to live successfully on Earth. He cannot help us as much as He could, if we don't read, praise and worship Him.

Quoting our Lord Jesus Christ, we must *"take heed"* and pay attention to those things that we sometimes consider as unimportant. Please take this Scripture seriously, and meditate on it all the time;

*"This Book of the Law shall not depart from your mouth, but you shall meditate in it day and night, that you may observe to do according to all that is written in it. For then you will make your way prosperous, and then you will have good success"* Joshua 1:8.

Many of the unpleasant and sad situations that are currently going on in our world today can only be dealt with through spiritual measures. Let's pay attention to this important point; the divine nature of human beings will make them to produce a rich harvest of good seed, if good seed are sown into their lives. It is now time to replace the unholy seed that has been sown into many people's lives with Pure Seed, which is the Word of God.

*"...I will put My laws in their mind and write them on their hearts; and I will be their God, and they shall be My people"*
Hebrews 8:10.

It's also important to note that if we willfully live outside of God's Instructions, there are spiritual consequences.

*"For he who sows to his flesh will of the flesh reap corruption..."* Galatians 6:8.

As said earlier, we need to seek God more than our usual methods. There's also the need for us to pray and confess positively on our land so that God can sanctify it. (There are some Prayer Points on Page 101).

After we have accepted Jesus Christ as our Lord and Savior, the Church Teachings and our Daily Devotions are what God will use to build up our Spirit Man. If we devote more time to the studying of the Scriptures, our hearts will be renewed, and our spiritual eyes will be opened to more spiritual truths. We will then become more sensitive to the things that we have previously not been paying attention to.

Furthermore, when we are consistent with our Daily Devotions, God will (through the Scriptures and our worship), make our hearts to be malleable, so that we can follow His Instructions. We will also be able to perceive His convictions when we are about to do the things that are not acceptable to Him.

*"And do not be conformed to this world, but be transformed by the renewing of your mind, that you may prove what is that good and acceptable and perfect will of God"* Romans 12:2.

Always remember that the Anointing will supply us with the necessary Spiritual Strength to deal with many of life's difficult situations. But this is not automatic; we must be committed to reading the Scriptures and seeking God and not wait until we have problems before doing something. Prevention, they say, is better than cure.

Furthermore, if we continuously strive for God's presence and pray more than our usual methods, as well as praying for others, more of His power will be drawn to us, our friends, relatives, and our communities, which will reduce or prevent most of the unpleasant things from happening around us.

*"If My people who are called by My name will humble themselves, and pray and seek My face, and turn from their*

> *wicked ways, then I will hear from heaven, and will forgive their sin and heal their land"*
> 2 Chronicles 7:14.

Please continue to pray and intercede for your relatives and friends that are in the World, and those that are vulnerable or in backslidden states. God will reward your efforts.

> *"…I sought for a man among them who would make a wall, and stand in the gap before Me on behalf of the land…"* Ezekiel 22:30.

As said earlier, if you are experiencing increased afflictions, especially after you have become consistent with your daily devotions, don't worry or give up. The reason for this is because your enemies know that your salvation is near, and they are trying to frustrate your efforts as you are trying to get closer to God.

I will suggest that you should also increase the amount of Scriptures that you are reading as well as your praise and worship, as this will increase your spiritual strengthen. Always remember that Christians are in a continuous spiritual warfare. Therefore, create an atmosphere of continuous worship to counter your spiritual enemies' effects.

As said earlier, strive to keep sin out of your life. When you do this, you will have the Anointing around you most of the time, hear God clearly, and you will be more than a conqueror in any situation that you may find yourself.

> *"And the ransomed of the LORD shall return,*
> *And come to Zion with singing,*
> *With everlasting joy on their heads.*
> *They shall obtain joy and gladness,*
> *And sorrow and sighing shall flee away"*
> Isaiah 35:10.

# *Is Your Soul Saved?*

If you have not invited Jesus Christ as your Lord and Savior, this is the time to do so. This is because you need the help of the Holy Spirit. He is our Guide and Comforter in life. He can only come to you after you have invited Jesus Christ, and when you begin to Study the Scriptures, praise, and worship God. You also need Him to help you to pray.

*"…If you confess with your mouth the Lord Jesus and believe in your heart that God has raised Him from the dead, you will be saved. For with the heart one believes unto righteousness, and with the mouth confession is made unto salvation"* Romans 10:9-10.

Please say the Prayer below:

*Dear Heavenly Father, I am sorry for my sins. Please forgive me. Jesus Christ, please come into my life and help me. In Your name I pray. Amen.*

It is important that you follow these Instructions:

**Prayer**
Pray every morning and ask God to protect and order your steps throughout the day. Also, ask the Holy Spirit to reveal your Divine Purpose to you. As you do, He will

begin to order your steps and lead you to where you are supposed to be in life.

**Read the Bible and Worship**
It's important that you create time for your Daily Devotion with God. When you're about to start your Daily Devotion (twice daily is advised), saying the Scripture below will help you. Also, pray and ask the Holy Spirit to teach you, as you study:

*"...He opened their understanding, that they might comprehend the Scriptures"* Luke 24:45.

As soon as you become a Christians, you are like a new born baby that requires milk. Likewise, our Souls require spiritual nourishments for it to develop. Therefore, reading the Bible and Praise and Worshipping God will provide the spiritual nourishments that your Soul requires. It will also protect you from 'spiritual infections', ease your pains if you are spiritually afflicted, as well as allow the Holy Spirit to come close and help you.

It's very important that you read the Bible every day but must be accompanied by Gospel Praise and Worship Music, or songs of adoration to God. This will draw the Holy Spirit to your situation quicker. I will advise you to incorporate reading the Book of Psalms during your Daily Devotion.

Reading the Bible generously will also help you to discern spiritual truth about your life and situations.

> *"I have more understanding than all my teachers,*
> *For Your testimonies are my meditation.*
> *I understand more than the ancients,*
> *Because I keep Your precepts"* Psalm 119:99-100.

As you study, get use to writing Scriptures on small/index cards to meditate on, memorize, and confess, during the day. This will help to protect your mind and strengthen you against temptations.

**Go to Church and Fellowship**
We are commanded to fellowship with other Christians. But it's important to ask the Holy Spirit to lead you to a Church.

> *"...Let us consider one another in order to stir up love and good works, not forsaking the assembling of ourselves together, as is the manner of some, but exhorting one another"* Hebrews 10:24-25.

One of the major reasons for going to Church is because Corporate Anointing is sometimes required for certain breakthroughs and this is only possible in a church environment. You need the prayers of other Christians and the Pastor. (The Bible says, *One person will chase a thousand and two are capable of putting ten thousand to flight;* Deuteronomy 32:30).

Secondly, the Church is the Holy Spirit School and Classroom. This is where He teaches us, His Students. The Pastors/Ministers are His Mouthpiece. You need a good and experienced Pastor that has been trained by the Holy Spirit, especially if you perceive that you have a major mission to accomplish in life. God will use the Pastor of the Church to train you for your future Ministry or Divine Calling for your life. Therefore, it's important that you pray and ask the Holy Spirit to direct you to His choice of Church for you.

**Baptism**
Get baptized in your local church. Christians are commanded to do so in the Bible;

> *"...Let every one of you be baptized in the name of Jesus Christ for the remission of sins; and you shall receive the gift of the Holy Spirit"* Acts 2:38.

**Serve**
As soon as you begin to attend your new Church, volunteer yourself as a worker in any of the Ministries. Also, pray for guidance to serve in the area of ministry that will be of great benefit to your future.

## Ask for Guidance
It's also important to always ask the Holy Spirit to guide you in everything that you do, so that He can help you to prevent mistakes. You are permitting Him to help you if you ask. God is the Owner of our lives and the Earth that we live in. We will be operating in the dark if we do not pray or acknowledge Him in all our ways, we are likely to make some mistakes, which are preventable.

*"The earth is the LORD's, and all its fullness,
The world and those who dwell therein"*
Psalm 24:1.

*"In all your ways acknowledge Him,
And He shall direct your paths"*
Proverbs 3:6.

## Love One Another
Love people as we are commanded and try your best to avoid malice and unforgiveness, so your prayers are not hindered. Use Isaiah 40:29 to pray for help if you're struggling in this area.

*"A new commandment I give to you, that you love one another; as I have loved you, that you also love one another. By this all will know that you are My disciples, if you have love for one another"* John 13:34-35.

Get Cleansed and Fill Your Lamp with Oil        Christy Tola

Please remember to share the Gospel with your relatives and friends.

God bless you.

# Prayers Points

# Scriptures for Prayers Points

*"It shall come to pass That before they call, I will answer; And while they are still speaking, I will hear"* Isaiah 65:24.

*"...Behold, I create new heavens and a new earth; And the former shall not be remembered or come to mind"* Isaiah 65:17.

*"...I will make them one nation in the land, on the mountains of Israel; and one king shall be king over them all; they shall no longer be two nations, nor shall they ever be divided into two kingdoms again"* Ezekiel 37:22.

*"I will deliver them from all their dwelling places in which they have sinned, and will cleanse them. Then they shall be My people, and I will be their God"* Ezekiel 37:23.

*"...Your descendants will inherit the nations, And make the desolate cities inhabited"* Isaiah 54:3.

"...The Lord will pass over the door and not allow the destroyer to come into your houses to strike you" Exodus 12:23.

"...The LORD will take away from you all sickness, and will afflict you with none of the terrible diseases of Egypt which you have known" Deuteronomy 7:15.

"He makes wars cease to the end of the earth; He breaks the bow and cuts the spear in two; He burns the chariot in the fire" Psalm 46:9.

"...He will turn
The hearts of the fathers to the children,
And the hearts of the children to their fathers..." Malachi 4:6.

"I lay down and slept;
I awoke, for the LORD sustained me" Psalm 3:5.

"Let all things be done decently and in order" 1 Corinthians 14:40.

"...Have mercy on me, and hear my prayer" Psalm 4:1.

"There will be abundance of grain in the earth..." Psalm 72:16.

> *"To You, O LORD, I lift up my soul.*
> *O my God, I trust in You;*
> *Let me not be ashamed;*
> *Let not my enemies triumph over me"* Psalm 25:1-2.

## General Prayers

Let our sins be forgiven
Let there be divine order of things in our day to day activities
Let the love of God reign in our midst
Let the spiritual eyes of understanding of many people be opened
Let the Angel of the LORD encompass all around us and deliver us
Let there be unity in our midst
Let people who are well-to-do share their wealth and resources
Let more people begin to use their talents to make profits
Let all the resources that we will need to maximize our potentials be provided for us
Let more jobs be created for the unemployed
Let us be linked with those who will help us to fulfill our divine purpose in life
Let those that are tormented by physical and spiritual enemies be delivered
Let hindrances be removed from our paths

Let pain and sorrow be a thing of the past in our lives
Let us be protected from our enemies
Let the power of our enemies be suppressed
Let the bereaved be consoled
Let us be helped not to stumble

## Prayers for Our Children

Let our children be protected
Let the fear of the Lord be in their hearts
Let divine intelligence be imparted to them
Let their hearts be drawn to God
Let morality be restored among our youth
Let there be peace and order in their schools
Let divine assistance be rendered to troubled schools
Let divine assistance be rendered to troubled children and their families
Let distant fathers begin to return to their children
Let some of our children that are experiencing negative peer pressure be divinely helped
Let those that are tempted to do the wrong things be divinely strengthened to resist
Let the hearts of those pressurizing others to do the wrong things be changed
Let the captives be set free
Let divine assistance be rendered to those wrongly convicted or imprisoned

## Prayers for Our Nations

Let there be more of God's Anointing to disperse the world's darkness
Let the Nation's Leaders begin to thirst for righteousness
Let those running the governments in various nations discharge their duties with the fear of the Lord
Let the people begin to thirst more for righteousness all over the world
Let covetousness be curbed among the people
Let divine wisdom be imparted to them to discharge their duties
Let more divine wisdom be impacted to various companies across the World
Let wisdom for godly games be released to companies manufacturing them
Let there be peace among the Nations
Let there be order in our land
Let there be peace in our communities
Let the people have progressive mindset
Let it rain in dry places
By divine favor, let the earth yield her increase in places where they are experiencing famine
Let the places that are prone to earthquakes be divinely helped
Let the places that are prone to sink holes be saturated with spiritual stones

Let there be divine assistance in areas that are experiencing destructive fires
Let the fires begin to subside
Let our weather generally begin to be favorable
Let there be more charitable organizations for the needy, especially in the areas of foods, housing and medicine.

In Jesus Name. Amen.

## Self-Help Pages

### Day 1

**Bible: Book (s) and Number of Chapters Read**

_____
_____
_____
_____

**Scriptures for Sowing**

_____
_____
_____
_____

**Scripture for Meditation**

_____
_____
_____
_____

**Scripture for Memorization**

_____
_____
_____
_____

## Day 2

**Bible: Book (s) and Number of Chapters Read**

_____
_____
_____
_____

**Scriptures for Sowing**

_____
_____
_____
_____
_____

**Scripture for Meditation**

_____
_____
_____

**Scripture for Memorization**

_____
_____
_____
_____

## Day 3

**Bible: Book (s) and Number of Chapters Read**

_____
_____
_____

**Scriptures for Sowing**

_____
_____
_____
_____
_____

**Scripture for Meditation**

_____
_____
_____

**Scripture for Memorization**

_____
_____
_____
_____

## Day 4

**Bible: Book (s) and Number of Chapters Read**

_____

_____

_____

**Scriptures for Sowing**

_____

_____

_____

_____

**Scripture for Meditation**

_____

_____

_____

**Scripture for Memorization**

_____

_____

_____

## Day 5

**Bible: Book (s) and Number of Chapters Read**

_____
_____
_____

**Scriptures for Sowing**

_____
_____
_____
_____
_____

**Scripture for Meditation**

_____
_____
_____

**Scripture for Memorization**

_____
_____
_____

## Day 6

## Bible: Book (s) and Number of Chapters Read

_____
_____
_____
_____

## Scriptures for Sowing

_____
_____
_____
_____
_____

## Scripture for Meditation

_____
_____
_____

## Scripture for Memorization

_____
_____
_____
_____

## Day 7

## Bible: Book (s) and Number of Chapters Read

_____
_____
_____
_____

## Scriptures for Sowing

_____
_____
_____
_____
_____

## Scripture for Meditation

_____
_____
_____
_____

## Scripture for Memorization

_____
_____
_____
_____
_____

## Day 8

### Bible: Book (s) and Number of Chapters Read

_____
_____
_____
_____

### Scriptures for Sowing

_____
_____
_____
_____
_____

### Scripture for Meditation

_____
_____
_____

### Scripture for Memorization

_____
_____
_____
_____

# Day 9

## Bible: Book (s) and Number of Chapters Read

_____
_____
_____

## Scriptures for Sowing

_____
_____
_____
_____
_____

## Scripture for Meditation

_____
_____
_____

## Scripture for Memorization

_____
_____
_____
_____
_____

## Day 10

**Bible: Book (s) and Number of Chapters Read**

_____

_____

_____

_____

**Scriptures for Sowing**

_____

_____

_____

_____

_____

**Scripture for Meditation**

_____

_____

_____

**Scripture for Memorization**

_____

_____

_____

_____

## Day 11

**Bible: Book (s) and Number of Chapters Read**

_____
_____
_____
_____

**Scriptures for Sowing**

_____
_____
_____
_____
_____
_____

**Scripture for Meditation**

_____
_____
_____
_____

**Scripture for Memorization**

_____
_____
_____
_____
_____

## Day 12

## Bible: Book (s) and Number of Chapters Read

_____
_____
_____
_____

## Scriptures for Sowing

_____
_____
_____
_____
_____

## Scripture for Meditation

_____
_____
_____

## Scripture for Memorization

_____
_____
_____
_____

## Day 13

**Bible: Book (s) and Number of Chapters Read**

_____
_____
_____

**Scriptures for Sowing**

_____
_____
_____
_____
_____

**Scripture for Meditation**

_____
_____
_____

**Scripture for Memorization**

_____
_____
_____
_____
_____

## Day 14

**Bible: Book (s) and Number of Chapters Read**

_____

_____
_____
_____

**Scriptures for Sowing**

_____

_____
_____
_____
_____

**Scripture for Meditation**

_____

_____
_____

**Scripture for Memorization**

_____

_____
_____
_____

## Day 15

## Bible: Book (s) and Number of Chapters Read

_____
_____
_____

## Scriptures for Sowing

_____
_____
_____
_____
_____

## Scripture for Meditation

_____
_____
_____
_____

## Scripture for Memorization

_____
_____
_____
_____
_____

## Day 16

**Bible: Book (s) and Number of Chapters Read**

_____
_____
_____
_____

**Scriptures for Sowing**

_____
_____
_____
_____
_____

**Scripture for Meditation**

_____
_____
_____
_____

**Scripture for Memorization**

_____
_____
_____
_____

## Day 17

### Bible: Book (s) and Number of Chapters Read

_____
_____
_____
_____

### Scriptures for Sowing

_____
_____
_____
_____
_____

### Scripture for Meditation

_____
_____
_____

### Scripture for Memorization

_____
_____
_____
_____

## Day 18

## Bible: Book (s) and Number of Chapters Read

_____
_____
_____
_____

## Scriptures for Sowing

_____
_____
_____
_____
_____
_____

## Scripture for Meditation

_____
_____
_____
_____

## Scripture for Memorization

_____
_____
_____
_____
_____

## Day 19

## Bible: Book (s) and Number of Chapters Read

_____
_____
_____

## Scriptures for Sowing

_____
_____
_____
_____
_____

## Scripture for Meditation

_____
_____
_____
_____

## Scripture for Memorization

_____
_____
_____
_____

## Day 20

### Bible: Book (s) and Number of Chapters Read

_____
_____
_____
_____

### Scriptures for Sowing

_____
_____
_____
_____
_____

### Scripture for Meditation

_____
_____
_____

### Scripture for Memorization

_____
_____
_____
_____

## Day 21

### Bible: Book (s) and Number of Chapters Read

_____
_____
_____
_____

### Scriptures for Sowing

_____
_____
_____
_____
_____
_____

### Scripture for Meditation

_____
_____
_____
_____

### Scripture for Memorization

_____
_____
_____
_____
_____

## Day 22

**Bible: Book (s) and Number of Chapters Read**

_____
_____
_____
_____

**Scriptures for Sowing**

_____
_____
_____
_____
_____

**Scripture for Meditation**

_____
_____
_____
_____

**Scripture for Memorization**

_____
_____
_____
_____

## Day 23

**Bible: Book (s) and Number of Chapters Read**

_____
_____
_____
_____

**Scriptures for Sowing**

_____
_____
_____
_____
_____

**Scripture for Meditation**

_____
_____
_____

**Scripture for Memorization**

_____
_____
_____
_____

## Day 24

### Bible: Book (s) and Number of Chapters Read

_____
_____
_____
_____

### Scriptures for Sowing

_____
_____
_____
_____
_____

### Scripture for Meditation

_____
_____
_____
_____

### Scripture for Memorization

_____
_____
_____
_____

**Day 25**

**Bible: Book (s) and Number of Chapters Read**

_____
_____
_____

**Scriptures for Sowing**

_____
_____
_____
_____
_____

**Scripture for Meditation**

_____
_____
_____

**Scripture for Memorization**

_____
_____
_____
_____

## Day 26

### Bible: Book (s) and Number of Chapters Read

_____
_____
_____
_____

### Scriptures for Sowing

_____
_____
_____
_____
_____

### Scripture for Meditation

_____
_____
_____

### Scripture for Memorization

_____
_____
_____
_____

## Day 27

**Bible: Book (s) and Number of Chapters Read**

_____
_____
_____
_____

**Scriptures for Sowing**

_____
_____
_____
_____
_____
_____

**Scripture for Meditation**

_____
_____
_____

**Scripture for Memorization**

_____
_____
_____
_____
_____

## Day 28

**Bible: Book (s) and Number of Chapters Read**

_____

_____

_____

**Scriptures for Sowing**

_____

_____

_____

_____

**Scripture for Meditation**

_____

_____

_____

**Scripture for Memorization**

_____

_____

_____

## Day 29

**Bible: Book (s) and Number of Chapters Read**

_____
_____
_____

**Scriptures for Sowing**

_____
_____
_____
_____

**Scripture for Meditation**

_____
_____
_____

**Scripture for Memorization**

_____
_____
_____
_____

## Day 30

### Bible: Book (s) and Number of Chapters Read

_____
_____
_____

### Scriptures for Sowing

_____
_____
_____
_____

### Scripture for Meditation

_____
_____
_____

### Scripture for Memorization

_____
_____
_____
_____

## Contact Details:

Christy Tola Arts & Books
P O Box 4243
Oak Park
IL 60304. USA.

Email: contact@tolabooks.com

More information about Pastor Christy Tola @ christytolaministries.org.

Facebook: Facebook.com/Christytolaministries

Youtube: Christy Tola Ministries

Instagram: Christy Tola

The Paperback Edition of 'Get Cleansed and Fill Your Lamp with Oil' and other Books by Christy Tola are now available at Amazon.com and other leading Bookstores.

THIS BOOK MUST NOT BE RE-EDITED.

Get Cleansed and Fill Your Lamp with Oil					Christy Tola